ADRENALINE RUSH

SNOWBOARDING

YVONNE THORPE

A⁺

Smart Apple Media

Published by Smart Apple Media,
an imprint of Black Rabbit Books
P.O. Box 3263, Mankato, Minnesota 56002
www.blackrabbitbooks.com

Printed in Printed in the United States
of America at Corporate Graphics,
North Mankato, Minnesota.

Published by arrangement with the
Watts Publishing Group LTD, London.

Library of Congress Cataloging-in-Publication Data

Thorpe, Yvonne.
Snowboarding / Yvonne Thorpe.
p. cm.—(Adrenaline rush)
Includes index.
Summary: "Explains the basics of snowboarding,
including the various styles of snowboarding, the
kinds of equipment needed, and the places where
snowboarding can be done. Includes biographies
of famous snowboarders and descriptions of
competitions featuring snowboarding events,
such as the X Games and Olympics"—Provided
by publisher.
ISBN 978-1-59920-686-8 (library binding)
1. Snowboarding—Juvenile literature. I. Title.
GV857.S57T47 2013
796.939—dc23

　　　　　　　　　　2011034067

PO1433
2-2012

9 8 7 6 5 4 3 2 1

Picture credits:
t–top, b–bottom, l–left, r–right, c–center
front cover Aleksey Ipatov/Dreamstime.com,
back cover jacomstephens/istockphoto.com,
1 Ben Renard-wiart/ Dreamstime.com, 4-5 Iland/
Dreamstime.com, 4bl Julia Pivovarova/ Dream-
stime.com, 6–7 Sports Illustrated/Getty Images,
7br Ustyujanin/ Shutterstock, 8–9 Viappy/ Dream-
stime.com, 8br Eugene Zhulkov/ Dreamstime.com,
9bl WireImage/ Getty, 10–11 Fotum / Dream-
stime.com, 11tl Galyna Andrushko/ Dreamstime.
com, 11tr Vanessa Morosini/ istockphoto.com,
12–13 Tudorica Alexandru/ Dreamstime.com, 13tr
Lenkas/ Dreamstime.com, 13br Aaron Settipane/
Dreamstime.com, 14–15 VVO/Shutterstock, 15tl
Melanie Horne/ Dreamstime.com, 16–17 Klorklor/
Dreamstime.com, 17tl Sam Downes/ Dreamstime.
com, 17c Ervin Monn / Shutterstock.com,
18–19 Getty Images, 19cr Maxim Petrichuk/
Dreamstime.com, 19bl WireImage/ Getty,
20–21 Brian Finestone/ Dreamstime.com, 21tr
Ben Renard-wiart/ Dreamstime.com, 21br Benis
Arapovic/ Dreamstime.com, 22 Galina Barskaya/
Dreamstime.com, 23tl Monkey Business Images/
Dreamstime.com, 23bl Getty Images, 24–25 Evg-
eny VasenevVV/ Shutterstock/ 24br Marlene Ford/
Dreamstime.com, 27br Ilya Postnikov/ Dream-
stime.com, Roca / Shutterstock.com,
28bl marc fischer/istockphoto.com.

Disclaimer
The website addresses (URLs) included in this
book were valid at the time of going to press.
However, because of the nature of the Internet,
it is possible that some addresses have changed,
or sites may have changed or closed down since
publication. While the author and publisher regret
any inconvenience this may cause to readers, no
responsibility for any such changes can be
accepted either by the author or the publisher.

In preparation of this book, all due care has been
exercised with regard to the advice, activities,
and techniques depicted. The publishers regret
that they can accept no liability for any loss or
injury sustained. When learning a new activity, it
is important to get expert advice and to follow a
manufacturer's instructions.

Words in **bold** are in the glossary on page 30.

CONTENTS

Hurling yourself down a mountain on a snowboard is more than exciting. When you can snowboard without falling over, you will definitely look really cool on the slopes. Throw in some awe-inspiring jumps and turns, and you are set to impress!

The Joy of Snowboarding

What is it that makes snowboarding so popular? This snow sport is super fun from the moment you first strap a board to your feet:

- learning—at first, you will spend most of your time falling over. But if you find some soft snow and do this with friends, even falling over can be a good time.

- improving—pretty soon you will learn to turn. As the board slides in an easy zig-zag across the slopes, the excitement will bring a big smile to your face.

A gentle slope like this one is great for learning to snowboard.

- showing off—when you are really good, you will be able to do jumps or carve through deep powder. The feeling of speed makes you feel like a snow-borne rocket man—or woman! This is one extreme sport where as many females as males take part.

Snowboarding World

You can snowboard anywhere there is snow. Some dedicated riders follow winter around the world, spending December to March in Europe or North America and June to September in South America or New Zealand. Others trek to icy glaciers in the middle of summer to get their boarding kicks.

After just a few weeks of learning, you could be pulling aerial tricks like this one.

Top Three Snowboarding Movies
- The Haakonsen Faktor—made in 1999, so a little old, this film features legendary Norwegian rider Terje Haakonsen. Shaun White (see page 13) says this is his favorite sports film ever.
- Neverland—this 2009 film has some of the best freeride sequences and riders around, as well as some amazing footage of urban snowboarding.
- Lame—ignore the title, this winner of the 2003–2004 Snowboarder Magazine *Video of the Year* award is anything but lame.

Snowboarding is so popular now that it is hard to imagine a time when it did not exist. But the sport is just a baby compared to skiing, its main rival on the slopes. People have been skiing for fun for more than 150 years, but snowboarding really took off only in the 1980s.

From Snurfer to Snowboard

During the 1970s, a lot of people rode "Snurfers." The name is a combination of "snow" and "surfer." The boards were like mini surfboards with leashes on the **nose**, which you could hold onto for balance and control. At the World Snurfer Championships in 1979, Jake Burton Carpenter turned up with a new kind of board. He had added straps that allowed him to attach the board to his boots. Today, many people recognize this as the first-ever snowboard.

Jake Burton Carpenter, sometimes called the "Godfather of Snowboarding," riding the powder near his home in New England.

Snowboard Heroes: Early Manufacturers
• Jake Burton Carpenter—*the Burton snowboard company was one of the first manufacturers, and today is the world's largest.*
• Tom Sims—*the skateboarder-turned-snowboarder organized the first-ever half-pipe world championship in 1983, and his company Sims produced many of the first boards.*
• Mike Olsen—*Olsen's GNU snowboard company was another of the early board manufacturers.*

"Ban this dangerous sport!"

The first snowboards were hard to control and tended to go downhill wildly. Their riders were often wild, too, and it was not long before snowboarding had a bad name. It was thought that snowboarding was dangerous and that it damaged ski **runs**. Many resorts banned snowboarding, and in the mid-1980s it was allowed in fewer than one in ten ski areas. The sport refused to die out, though, and by 1990, resorts began to create separate areas for snowboarding.

Not long ago, most ski resorts tried to keep skiers and snowboarders separate.

Snowboarding has changed a lot since the early days. Now, snowboarders are welcome just about everywhere. Not everything has changed, of course— snowboarders are still united by the thrill of sliding over snow. And unfortunately, they still have to use uncomfortable lifts designed for skiers.

Styles of Snowboarding

Once they have learned the basics, most riders specialize in a particular type of riding. The biggest division is between freestyle and freeride:

- freestylers make the most of any chance they get to become airborne or to slide their board along an obstacle. Their riding style is often influenced by skateboarding, and they practice in snow parks, which are the wintersports equivalent of skate parks. Freestylers are often found trudging to the top of a half-pipe or swooshing down it.

- freeriders are most interested in carving out big turns, riding the whole mountain from top to bottom. They do jumps but usually only when the terrain allows—for example, when the only way down is to leap off a cliff and land in the soft snow beneath. Freeriders are often found waiting for either the first or last lift of the day, hoping for a clear run at the slopes.

Deep powder snow like this is snowboarding heaven if you like backcountry freeriding.

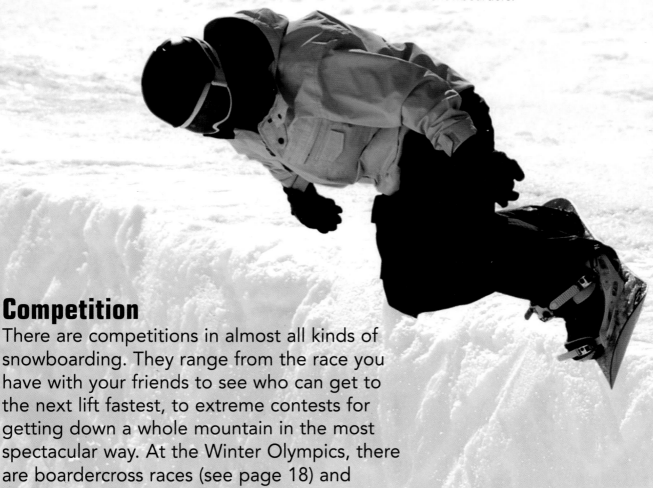

You can see from the gouges in its side that this half-pipe has been ridden by a lot of freestyle snowboarders.

Competition

There are competitions in almost all kinds of snowboarding. They range from the race you have with your friends to see who can get to the next lift fastest, to extreme contests for getting down a whole mountain in the most spectacular way. At the Winter Olympics, there are boardercross races (see page 18) and half-pipe contests (see page 16).

Cara-Beth Burnside was one of the first women to show that female riders can be just as awesome in the half-pipe as men. Originally a skateboarder (and winner of Female Skater of the Year in 2003), she is one of a tiny group of people who have won gold medals at both Summer and Winter X Games.

CARA-BETH BURNSIDE

Snowboarding equipment is pretty simple. Boarders just need a board, boots, and bindings. There are lots of different styles, from long **swallow-tail** powder boards to shorter freestyle boards. The boots and bindings vary as well.

Buying a Board

If you are new to boarding, you might want to rent a board at first. Once you know what kind of equipment you like, it might be a good idea to buy your own. Board shops will be able to give you advice on which board suits your riding style best.

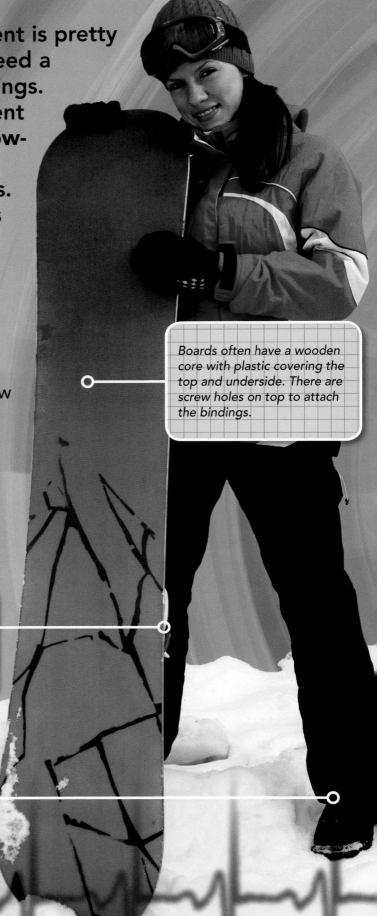

Boards often have a wooden core with plastic covering the top and underside. There are screw holes on top to attach the bindings.

Thin metal strips, called edges, run down the outside of the bottom. These are used to help the board grip into the snow while turning or stopping.

Boots are designed to be stiff enough to keep their shape during turns, and are padded so that they are comfortable to wear all day.

Bindings hold the boot to the board. Strap bindings, which grip the toe and ankle areas, are most common.

A short, lightweight board makes spins and tricks in the air easier.

Types of Boards

There are two basic types of boards:

- freestyle—for freestyle, people often ride shorter boards that come up to their chins when stood upright. These boards are double-ended. Boots tend to be less stiff to make twisting and spinning easier.

- freeride—freeride boarders use a longer board (up to their nose), and the nose (front) of the board is usually longer than the **tail**.

You could go boarding in shorts and a T-shirt (and some people do in spring). But when the chairlift stops moving because a sudden storm has closed in, you will regret it. Having the right clothes and equipment makes snowboarding much more enjoyable and safe.

Snowboard Clothes

The key to dressing for boarding is to wear layers so you can strip off a layer or two if you get hot. A standard outfit includes:

• thermal base layer, which draws away sweat and keeps you warm.

• pants, often with side-zips that can be opened if you get too hot. The best ones are waterproof with reinforced areas on the knees and bottom. They also have elastic cuffs that fit over your boots.

• thin fleece, ideally with a full-length zipper for cooling down and a high collar for keeping your neck warm.

• jacket, usually with a **snow skirt**.

In a crash like this one, a snow skirt inside your jacket stops snow from being shoved into areas where it should not be!

Other Equipment

All riders wear gloves to keep their hands warm and dry. Many snowboarders also ride wearing a helmet, goggles, and a small backpack (see below).

Snowboarding goggles stop the glare of the white snow from damaging your eyes.

Helmet
Rarely required, but as moves become increasingly trickier, more riders are choosing to wear them.

Backpack
Inside their backpack, most riders will have the following:
- *spare clothes.*
- *survival blanket and cell phone in case of an accident. Backcountry riders also carry* **avalanche** *gear, such as* **avalanche reflectors**.
- *multi-tool to make repairs and adjustments to the snowboard and the bindings.*
- *drinks to keep hydrated. Keep drinks in a soft plastic bottle, not a hard metal one.*
- *snacks in case of hunger and/or disaster.*

Sometimes called "The Flying Tomato" because of his red hair, Shaun White is probably the best half-pipe snowboarder the world has ever seen. He is the winner of multiple X Games gold medals (as well as a silver for skateboarding), but his biggest wins were at the Olympic Games. White won gold at the 2006 Turin Olympics, then again at the 2010 Vancouver Games.

SHAUN WHITE

13

Most boarders ride in ski resorts, where there are lifts that will take them to the top of the slope. Most of the time they then slide back downhill on a run, which is a specially prepared area of smoothed-out snow, free of obstacles.

Hill Markers and Grades

Runs are usually marked out with poles, trees, or other markers on either side of the slope. Even in heavy snow when it is hard to see, boarders and skiers can pick their way carefully down the mountain by following these markers.

In almost all the world's ski resorts, runs are graded according to difficulty. In North America, the basic grades go green, blue, and black. In Europe, the grades start with an easy green (in France only), then progress through blue, red, and black.

Lifts were designed with forward-facing skiers in mind, rather than sideways-riding snowboarders. As a result, they are often a very uncomfortable experience.

Your first ride on a T-bar lift like this one can be a humbling experience. People quickly get the hang of them, though.

Lifts

After sliding to the bottom of a slope, boarders hitch a ride back uphill on a ski lift. There are three main kinds of ski lifts:

- cable cars and gondolas are the easiest to get on and off and the most comfortable.

- chair lifts are somewhat easy to get on and off, but they force you to twist around uncomfortably to sit down.

- drag lifts, such as T-bar or pommel lifts, are hard to use and uncomfortable. They are a sign that a resort was not designed for snowboarders!

Top Snowboard Cell Phone Games
- *Snowboard Hero—a great basic game, with the chance to perform all kinds of mid-air tricks as you leap and slide your way down a choice of courses.*
- *Extreme Air Snowboarding—the great tutorial mode will soon have you ripping it up in the virtual half-pipe.*
- *X2 Snowboarding—one of the most popular snowboard games, which boasts amazing control and customization, and exciting runs.*

ON THE SCREEN

15

Many riders quickly find that simply sliding downhill is not enough for them. They want to make their friends gasp in amazement at their acrobatic skills. They want to make onlookers cheer at their bravery. They want to pull jaw-dropping tricks that will push them to the limit. They want, in two words, big air.

A rider gets big air off a custom-built ramp in Val d'Isere in the French Alps.

Half-Pipes and High Jumps

There are various ways to get airborne on a snowboard. You can even **pop** a little **ollie** (a small jump) while riding along flat ground. But to get high, you need a ramp. The bigger the ramp, the higher you can go. Skilled riders put together incredibly spectacular routines on half-pipes.

A half-pipe is a U-shaped ramp, just like those seen at a skate park. Competition riders have to concentrate on making one long, smooth run, usually with six or more jumps, rather than doing a single huge aerial. The half-pipe is not where the biggest jumps are seen.

Quarter-Pipes and Higher Jumps

A quarter-pipe is half of a half-pipe. The riders get a long run-up (sometimes towed behind a snowmobile for maximum speed), then launch vertically into the air. They get one chance, and all they have to do is land safely. In 2007, at the age of 33, Terje Haakonsen set a new world record for a quarter-pipe jump of 32.15 feet (9.8 m) above the top of the ramp.

Spectators crane their necks up to try to keep a big air competitor in view.

Snowboarding legend Kevin Pearce at the Open Snowboarding Championships in Laax, Switzerland, in 2009.

Air and Style
This is an annual aerial contest currently held in Innsbruck, Austria (it has also been held in Munich, Germany). The riders leap from a giant jump, performing their best tricks while airborne. Past champions have included some of snowboarding's greats: Ingmar Backmann, Terje Haakonsen, Stefan Gimpl, Shaun White, Travis Rice, and Kevin Pearce.

BOARDERCROSS

Boardercross was one of the biggest hits of the 2010 Winter Olympics in Vancouver, Canada. This might have been because it features many crashes and embarrassing mistakes, even by some of the world's best riders!

Competitors head for the line at the end of a boardercross contest. The blue line marks the edge of the run.

Side-by-Side Racing

Boardercross is a knockout competition. In each round, four riders race side-by-side over a series of jumps and obstacles. There is usually only one fast way down the course, and with four riders trying to fit themselves into it, things can get messy. The first two across the finish line go on to the next round. The last two across go home.

The boardercross style of competition is so popular that it has been borrowed by skiing. Ski cross is now one of the most popular skiing events.

18

Boardercross Courses

The course normally opens with a start gate. As soon as the gate opens opens, the riders fly out, trying to pick up as much speed as possible. Then there are a series of banked-up turns that test the riders' ability to corner at high speed. There are always a few jumps, too—sometimes really big ones. On beginner courses, you can ride around the jumps or take them slowly, but this takes a lot longer.

Whether you ride regular (left foot first) or goofy (right foot first), there will be some turns on a boardercross course that suit you—and some that do not!

US rider Lindsey Jacobellis is famous for two things: being one of the best female boardercross riders, and being one of the unluckiest. At the 2006 Olympics, Jacobellis was safely in the lead when, going into the second-to-last jump, she crashed. By the time she got up, she could only finish second. "Snowboarding is fun," she later said, "I was having fun."

LINDSEY JACOBELLIS

Once riders have mastered basic snowboarding skills (going in a straight line and turning), they start adding some extra freestyle tricks. Most experts have at least a handful of tricks that they can throw in at a split-second's notice if the terrain gives them the chance.

This boarder is performing an indy grab, with the leading arm thrown out behind for good measure.

Freestyle Tricks

Snowboarding tricks sometimes sound like a whole different language. A "McTwist," for example, is a forward-flipping backside 540 with a grab. But most tricks are made up of just three things—jumps, spins, and grabs:

• jumps—a simple jump can be done off ramps or bumps in the surface of the snow. Lots of people learn jumps using the little built-up areas at the edges of a run.

• spins—these add difficulty to a jump. Twisting around 180 degrees while in the air, for example, means riders land "fakie"—with the tail of the board in front.

- grabs—this is when you grab the nose, tail, or rail of the board while in the air. The most basic grab is an "indy," which involves grabbing the toe edge of the board between your feet using your trailing hand.

Expert freestyle boarders throw other moves into their routines, including:

- grinds—grinds involve sliding the board along handrails, roofs, and fallen trees.

- rolls—a roll is an experts-only move. Rolls involve getting upside-down, or inverted, while airborne. They are considered so dangerous that they have been banned in some competitions.

Freestyle aerial skills can come in handy when you are riding backcountry, too.

Top Two Snow Parks
- *Copper Mountain, Colorado—regularly voted one of North America's best snow parks, with something for every ability level.*
- *Snow Park, New Zealand—no prizes for imaginative naming, but this is a good place to spot some of the world's top freestyle snowboarders during the southern hemisphere winter.*

In the early days of snowboarding, if you wanted to snowboard, you had to do it away from marked runs. Today, many boarders still enjoy the feeling of ignoring the hill markers and finding their own way down the mountain. North Americans call this backcountry riding, but in Europe, this is known as off-piste riding.

A rider flies high on a backcountry jump.

Experts Only!

Freeriders need impressive skills because they have to be able to deal with whatever the mountain throws at them. A 16-foot (5 m) cliff? They will have to jump it, or stop in time to **backtrack**. Deep powder? Keep the nose of the board up, or dig themselves out. Thick forest? Make sure their turning technique is up to snuff!

Backcountry Hazards

Snowboarding away from marked runs is dangerous. Deep snow can hide all kinds of hazards, such as rocks, deep holes, and fallen trees. Away from the areas that have been made safe by groomers, there is always a danger that you could set off an avalanche.

Sometimes the powder is so deep, you just have to do a happy wheelie.

ON THE SCREEN

Top Freeride Movie That's It, That's All— a dream rider lineup of Travis Rice, Terje Haakonsen, Jeremy Jones, Nicolas Müller, Bryan Iguchi, and many more, with jaw-dropping results.

Ride with a Guide

The best way to ride backcountry is with a local guide. Guides can be hired for an hour or two, half a day, or a whole day. The main reasons for riding with a guide are:
• they know the areas where it is safe.
• they can take you on the best, most secret routes.
• a guide will stop you from going down a valley or slope that looks inviting, but just out of sight, turns into a river valley with no way out except to walk back up the mountain.

Travis Rice lives in Jackson Hole, Wyoming, one of the top freeride locations in the US. His riding combines the massive jumps and wild settings of freeriding with the technical skills of freestyle. Much in demand from filmmakers, Rice's most famous jump is probably a switch 540 performed while jumping 40 yards (37 m) across Chad's Gap in Utah.

TRAVIS RICE

Snowboarding is good for you. It makes your heart and lungs stronger, improves coordination and balance, and introduces you to places you might not otherwise see. But snowboarding is also a dangerous sport. Every year riders are seriously injured, or even killed.

Always take heed of the avalanche warnings, and avoid areas where there is a risk of avalanches.

Stay Safe

These simple things can make snowboarding safer:

- check your gear—make sure that all the screws and bolts on your bindings are tight. They are under massive pressure, and one popping off can be disastrous.

- wear a helmet—break an arm or leg, and a few months later, most people will have a full recovery. Head injuries are worse and can be fatal.

- go at your own speed—it can be tempting to try to keep up with better riders, but once you are moving too fast, things can go wrong more quickly than you would expect. Before you know it, you could be crashing into a tree you would normally be able to avoid.

Slope Rules

Ski resorts are often crowded, with people of all abilities sharing the slopes. To make things safer, snowboarders and skiers have come up with a few simple guidelines:

- *The downhill person has right of way. This means that if you are farther up the slope, you must safely avoid people below you as you pass them. If you cannot pass safely, slow down.*
- *Never stop in the middle of the run, or just over the brow of a slope where other riders cannot see you, for a picnic or a chat. Pull over to the side, where you will not be in anyone's way.*
- *Snowboarders must always wear a **leg leash**, so that their board cannot slide off down the slope and injure someone.*

- do not go unless you know the way—just because another boarder has taken a particular route, that does not mean it is safe to follow. The other boarder might be much more experienced than you—or could have crashed just around the corner!

This rider has gotten caught at the edge of a small avalanche. Even a small one like this will contain tons of snow, rock, and ice.

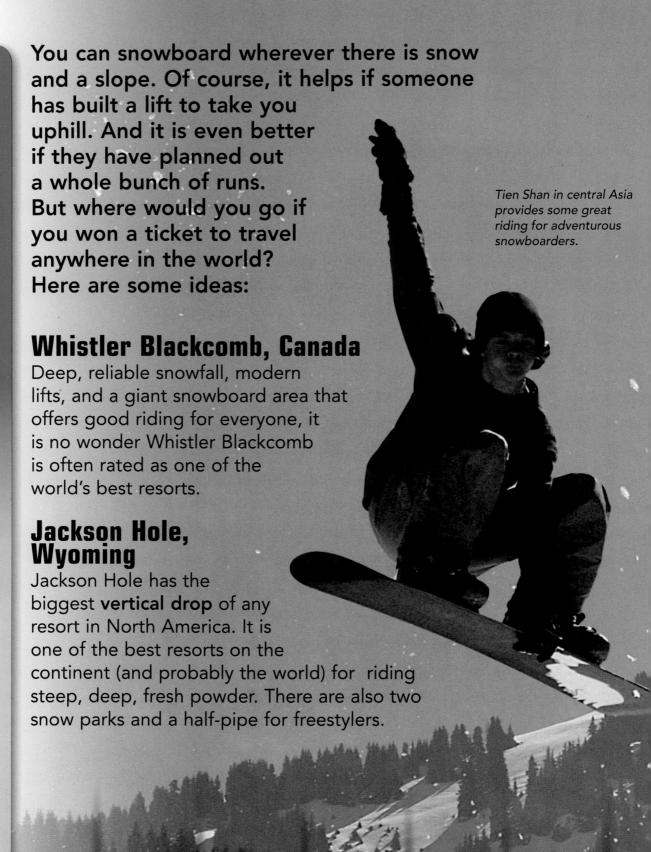

You can snowboard wherever there is snow and a slope. Of course, it helps if someone has built a lift to take you uphill. And it is even better if they have planned out a whole bunch of runs. But where would you go if you won a ticket to travel anywhere in the world? Here are some ideas:

Tien Shan in central Asia provides some great riding for adventurous snowboarders.

Whistler Blackcomb, Canada

Deep, reliable snowfall, modern lifts, and a giant snowboard area that offers good riding for everyone, it is no wonder Whistler Blackcomb is often rated as one of the world's best resorts.

Jackson Hole, Wyoming

Jackson Hole has the biggest **vertical drop** of any resort in North America. It is one of the best resorts on the continent (and probably the world) for riding steep, deep, fresh powder. There are also two snow parks and a half-pipe for freestylers.

Verbier, Switzerland

One of Europe's oldest ski resorts, this is the place to head for some of the best snowboarding through trees in Europe.

Queenstown, New Zealand

The adventure sports capital of New Zealand, Queenstown offers a massive variety of runs, from gentle slopes for beginners to some of the world's best **heli-boarding**.

Chamonix, France

For experienced backcountry riders, Chamonix is heaven. For anyone else, it is not so much fun. The extreme, steep slopes and regular falls of fresh snow mean that hard-core riders spend the whole winter here.

Åre, Sweden

Åre (pronounced "ore-uh") is so far north that in the middle of the winter, you need floodlights to find your way around the snow park. But at the end of the season, in May, the sun barely sets. If you want to snowboard in the light of the midnight sun, this is the place.

Snow parks such as this one in Almaty, Kazakhstan, are filled with riders throughout the winter.

Some snowboarders really do not like crowds. They gave up slope riding years ago. Even the popular backcountry areas have started to seem a bit too busy. What they really enjoy is having an entire mountain all to themselves (and perhaps a few friends). This is the world of extreme snowboarding.

Living the Dream

Imagine this: you and a few others load your boards on the helicopter's rack and climb in. The pilot takes off, and flies you to the top of an **untracked** slope of fresh powder. The drop-off point might be so small that the pilot cannot actually land. You may have to jump out of the chopper with your board!

The reward, however, is the ride down through fresh snow with no lift noises, no skiers, and no beginners to slow down for. At the bottom, the chopper is waiting to take you to the next drop-off.

This dream actually exists. It is called heli-boarding, and it can be done at many resorts. In other places, snowmobiles are used in the same way, to take riders to out-of-the-way locations. This can be a good option if you are not a millionaire, as it is much cheaper than heli-boarding.

Using a snowmobile to get up a mountain is pretty fun.

Remote Locations

Some riders have started exploring places where snowboarding and skiing have never been done before. They have to trek there using **snowshoes** or mountain-climbing boots with **crampons**. The amount of effort and equipment involved means that only a few expeditions like this take place each year.

Top Three Heli-Boarding Spots
- *Valdez, Alaska—possibly the spiritual home of heli-boarding, the Valdez Mountains offer some of the deepest, most reliable powder around.*
- *Queenstown, New Zealand—famous as an adrenaline-junkie's kind of town. In the winter you can get your fix by taking a helicopter to New Zealand's Southern Alps.*
- *Zermatt, Switzerland—Switzerland is probably the best country in Europe for heli-boarding, and Zermatt is surrounded by some extremely high mountains, including the world-famous Matterhorn.*

A short helicopter ride will take you to the parts of a mountain that ski lifts just cannot reach.

avalanche
a slide of huge amounts of snow down a mountainside.

avalanche reflectors
special patches, sewn into ski clothing and backpacks, which reflect radio waves and allow rescue teams to detect people trapped beneath snow.

backtrack
go back the way you came. This usually means walking back up the mountain.

crampons
spiky attachments for the soles of a boot, which allow it to grip the ice and snow.

heli-boarding
riding a helicopter to a remote drop-off point on a mountain to snowboard down.

leg leash
a strap attaching your leg to a snowboard.

nose
front end of a snowboard.

ollie
jump done from level ground, using the rider's speed and leg strength to get off the ground.

pop
to perform suddenly.

runs
marked areas on a slope for downhill skiing or snowboarding.

snow skirt
inner layer of a jacket that is tightened around the hips to keep snow from going up inside the jacket during a fall.

snowshoes
wide, lightweight platforms that can be strapped to your shoes to make it easier to walk across snow.

swallow-tail board
board with a tail that has two pointed tips.

tail
rear end of a snowboard.

untracked
without any signs of other snowboarders having passed.

vertical drop
distance from the top of the highest run to the bottom of the lowest.

Competitions
The World Cup
This is a season-long set of competitions that decides who were the best riders over the whole year. There are several different categories, including Big Air, Boardercross, and Half-Pipe. To find a World Cup event near you, go to www.fissnowboard.com.

X Games
The X Games is a US event held every year, and it attracts the world's top snowboarders. There are also other versions of the X Games, for example in Europe. Go to www.espn.go.com/snowboarding/

The Winter Olympics
The Olympics is the largest international competition. Go to www.olympic.org/snowboard for information about the events, past medalists, and the history of the sport.

Online Magazines
http://fresh.snowboardermag.com
The online resource of the US print magazine *Snowboarder*, with excellent articles and videos about travel locations, equipment, techniques, and top snowboarders.

http://whitelines.mpora.com
Visit the online world of *Whitelines* snowboard magazine from the UK with interviews, equipment and techniques, plus videos. A good take on the European snowboarding scene.

http://www.boardtheworld.com
A purely online magazine, with excellent coverage of the international competition scene. Also carries resort information for just about every resort you can think of.

INDEX

28.50

10/24/12